SIDE BY SIDE

English Through Guided Conversations

2B

Steven J. Molinsky

Bill Bliss

Illustrated by

Richard E. Hill

Prentice-Hall Inc., Englewood Cliffs, New Jersey 07632

Library of Congress Cataloging in Publication Data

MOLINSKY, STEVEN J.
    Side by Side

    Includes indexes.
      1. English language—Conversation and phrase books.
    2. English language—Text books for foreign speakers.
    I. Bliss, Bill.   II. Title.
    PE1131.M58   1983   428.3′4   82-20425
    ISBN 0-13-809798-4 (Book 2B)

© 1983 by Prentice-Hall, Inc., Englewood Cliffs, N.J. 07632

Printed in the United States of America

10   9

Editorial/production supervisor: Penelope Linskey
Art/camera copy supervisor: Diane Heckler-Koromhas
Cover design by Suzanne Behnke
Manufacturing buyer: Harry P. Baisley

0-13-809798-4

PRENTICE-HALL INTERNATIONAL, INC., *London*
PRENTICE-HALL OF AUSTRALIA PTY. LIMITED, *Sydney*
EDITORA PRENTICE-HALL DO BRASIL, LTDA., *Rio de Janeiro*
PRENTICE-HALL OF CANADA, LTD., *Toronto*
PRENTICE-HALL OF INDIA PRIVATE LIMITED, *New Delhi*
PRENTICE-HALL OF JAPAN, INC., *Tokyo*
PRENTICE-HALL OF SOUTHEAST ASIA PTE. LTD., *Singapore*
WHITEHALL BOOKS LIMITED, WELLINGTON, *New Zealand*

Contents

BOOK 2A

Contents

BOOK **2B**

To the Teacher

Side by Side: Book Two is a conversational grammar book.

We do not seek to describe the language, nor prescribe its rules. Rather, we aim to help students learn to *use* the language grammatically, through practice with meaningful conversational exchanges.

This book is intended for adult and young-adult learners of English. It is designed to provide the intermediate-level student with the basic foundation of English grammar, through a carefully sequenced progression of conversational exercises and activities.

WHY A CONVERSATIONAL GRAMMAR BOOK?

Grammar is usually isolated and drilled through a variety of traditional structure exercises such as repetition, substitution, and transformation drills. Such exercises effectively highlight particular grammatical structures . . . but they are usually presented as a string of single sentences, not related to each other in any unifying, relevant context.

Traditional dialogues, on the other hand, may do a fine job of providing examples of real speech . . . but they don't usually offer sufficient practice with the structures being taught. Teachers and students are often frustrated by the lack of a clear grammatical focus in these meaningful contexts. Furthermore, it's hard to figure out what to *do* with a dialogue after you've read it, memorized it, or talked about it.

In this book we have attempted to combine the best features of traditional grammatical drills and contextually rich dialogues. The aim is to actively engage the students in meaningful conversational exchanges within carefully structured grammatical frameworks. The students are then encouraged to break away from the textbook and *use* these frameworks to create conversations *on their own*.

GRAMMATICAL PARADIGMS

Each lesson in the book covers one or more specific grammatical structures. A new structure appears first in the form of a grammatical paradigm, a simple schema of the structure.

These paradigms are to be a reference point for students as they proceed through the lesson's conversational activities. While these paradigms highlight the structures being taught, they are not intended to be goals in themselves.

We don't want our students simply to parrot back these rules: we want them to engage in conversations that show they can *use* them correctly.

GUIDED CONVERSATIONS

Guided Conversations are the dialogues and question-and-answer exchanges which are the primary learning devices in this book. Students are presented with a model conversation that highlights a specific aspect of the grammar. In the exercises that follow the model, students pair up and work "side by side," placing new content into the given conversational framework.

How to Introduce Guided Conversations

There are many ways to introduce these conversations. We don't want to dictate any particular method. Rather, we encourage you to develop strategies that are compatible with your own teaching style, the specific needs of your students, and the particular grammar and content of the lesson at hand.

Some teachers will want books closed at this stage, giving their students a chance to listen to the model before seeing it in print.

Other teachers will want students to have their books open for the model conversation or see it written on the blackboard. The teacher may read or act out the conversation while students follow along, or may read through the model with another student, or may have two students present the model to the class.

Whether books are open or closed, students should have ample opportunity to understand and practice the model before attempting the exercises that follow it.

How to Use Guided Conversations

In these conversational exercises, the students are asked to place new content into the grammatical and contextual framework of the model. The numbered exercises provide the student with new information which is "plugged into" the framework of the model conversation. Sometimes this framework actually appears as a "skeletal dialogue" in the text. Other times the student simply inserts the new information into the model that has just been practiced. (Teachers who have written the model conversation on the blackboard can create the skeletal dialogue by erasing the words that are replaced in the exercises.)

The teacher's key function is to pair up students for "side by side" conversational practice and then to serve as a resource to the class: for help with the structure, new vocabulary, and pronunciation.

"Side by side" practice can take many forms. Most teachers prefer to call on two students at a time to present a conversation to the class. Other teachers have their students pair up and practice the conversations together. Or small groups of students might work together, pairing up within these groups and presenting the conversations to each other.

This paired practice helps teachers address the varying levels of ability of their students. Some teachers like to pair stronger students with weaker ones. The slower student clearly gains through this pairing, while the more advanced student also strengthens his or her abilities by lending assistance to the speaking partner.

Other teachers will want to pair up or group students of *similar* levels of ability. In this arrangement, the teacher can devote greater attention to students who need it while giving more capable students the chance to learn from and assist each other.

While these exercises are intended for practice in conversation, teachers also find them useful as *writing* drills which reinforce oral practice and enable students to study more carefully the grammar highlighted in the conversations.

Once again, we encourage you to develop strategies that are most appropriate for your class.

The "Life Cycle" of a Guided Conversation

It might be helpful to define the different stages in the "life cycle" of a guided conversation.

I. *The Presentation Stage:*
The model conversation is introduced and is practiced by the class.

II. *The Rehearsal Stage:*
Immediately after practicing the model, students do the conversational exercises that follow it. For homework, they practice these conversations, and perhaps write out a few. Some lessons also ask students to create their own original conversations based on the model.

III. *The Performance Stage:*
The next day students do the conversational exercises in class, preferably with their textbooks and notebooks closed. Students shouldn't have to memorize these conversations. They will most likely remember them after sufficient practice in class and at home.

IV. The Incorporation Stage:
   The class reviews the conversation or reviews pieces of the conversation in the days that follow. With repetition and time, the guided conversation "dissolves" and its components are incorporated into the student's active language.

ON YOUR OWN

   An important component of each lesson is the On Your Own activity. These student-centered exercises reinforce the grammatical structures of the lesson while breaking away from the text and allowing students to contribute content of their own.
   These activities take various forms: role-plays, extended guided conversations, questions about the student's real world, and topics for classroom discussion and debate. In these exercises the students are asked to bring new content to the classroom, based on their interests, their backgrounds, and the farthest reaches of their imaginations.
   We recommend that the teacher read through these activities in class and assign them as homework for presentation the next day. In this way, students will automatically review the previous day's grammar while contributing new and inventive content of their own.
   On Your Own activities are meant for simultaneous grammar reinforcement and vocabulary building. Students should be encouraged to use a dictionary when preparing these exercises. Thus, they will use not only the words they know, but the words they would *like* to know in order to bring their own interests, backgrounds, and imaginations into the classroom. As a result, students will be teaching each other new vocabulary and also sharing a bit of their lives with others in the class.
   In conclusion, we have attempted to make the study of English grammar a lively and relevant experience for the student. While conveying to you the substance of our textbook, we hope that we have also conveyed the spirit: that learning the grammar can be conversational . . . student-centered . . . and fun.

Steven J. Molinsky
Bill Bliss

11

Passive Voice

Jim took this photograph.
This photograph **was taken** by Jim.

Read and practice.

A. This is really a good photograph of you.

B. I think so, too.

A. Who **took** it?

B. I'm not sure. I think it **was taken** by my Uncle George.

A. This is a very sad poem.

B. I think so, too.

A. Who **wrote** it?

B. I'm not sure. I think it **was written** by Shakespeare.

1. This is a very cute photograph of your children.
take

2. This is an excellent magazine article.
write

3. This is a beautiful sonata.
compose

4. This is really an exciting movie.
direct

5. This is a very funny political cartoon.
draw

6. This is a very fine portrait of you.
paint

7. This is a very useful machine.
invent

8. This is an impressive bridge.
build

9. This is a magnificent building.
design

10. This is a very talented elephant.
train

11. This is a very strange computer.
program

12. This is really a crazy fad.
begin

Somebody has fed the cat.
The cat **has been fed**.

Somebody has turned off the lights.
The lights **have been turned off**.

A. Do you want me to feed Rover?

B. No. Don't worry about it.
He's already **been fed**.

A. Do you want me to ring* the church bells?

B. No. Don't worry about it.
They've already **been rung**.

*ring–rang–rung

1. *make the bed*

2. *send the packages*

3. *do the dishes*

4. *sweep the porch*

5. *carve the turkey*

6. *hide*the Christmas presents*

7. *write down Mary's telephone number*

8. *freeze† the leftover chicken*

9. *take the garbage out*

10. *wake‡ the children up*

11. *teach two-word verbs today*

12. *sing the National Anthem*

*hide–hid–hidden
†freeze–froze–frozen
‡wake–woke–woken

A. Have you heard about Harry?

B. No, I haven't. What happened?

A. He **was fired** last week.

B. What a shame!*
That's the second time he**'s been fired** this year!

A. Have you heard about Helen?

B. No, I haven't. What happened?

A. She **was given** a raise last week.

B. That's great!†
That's the second time she**'s been given** a raise this year!

*You can also say: That's terrible!   That's too bad!
†You can also say: That's fantastic!   That's wonderful!

1. *Mr. and Mrs. Wilson*
robbed

2. *Uncle John*
invited to the White House

3. *Larry*
hurt in a car accident

4. *Maria*
promoted

5. *our mailman*
bitten* by a dog

6. *the man across the street*
arrested

7. *Claudia*
sent to Honolulu on business

8. *Mrs. Miller*
taken to the hospital by ambulance

9. *Arthur*
rejected by the army

10. *Lana*
offered a movie contract

11. *Walter*
chosen† "employee of the month"

12.

*bite–bit–bitten
†choose–chose–chosen

Somebody is repairing my car.
My car is **being repaired**.

A. Hello. Is this Joe's Auto Repair Shop?

B. Yes, it is. Can I help you?

A. Yes, please. This is Mrs. Jones.
I'm calling about my car.
Has it **been repaired** yet?

B. Not yet. It's **being repaired** right now.

A. Can I pick it up soon?

B. Yes. Come by at four o'clock.
I'm sure it'll be ready by then.

A. Hello. Is this _____'s _____?

B. Yes, it is. Can I help you?

A. Yes, please. This is _____.
I'm calling about my _____.
(Has it/Have they) been _____ yet?

B. Not yet. (It's/They're) being _____ right now.

A. Can I pick (it/them) up soon?

B. Yes. Come by at _____ o'clock.
I'm sure (it'll/they'll) be ready by then.

1. *watch*
   repair

2. *TV*
   fix

3. *pants*
   take in

4. *poodle*
   clip

5. *will*
   rewrite

6.

ON YOUR OWN

> Answers **should be written** in your notebook.
> Students **should be required** to take an examination.
> Smoking **shouldn't be allowed** in the classroom.

WHAT'S YOUR OPINION?

Talk about these issues with other students in your class.

1. **Should** your native language **be spoken** during the English class?

2. **Should** students **be allowed** to use dictionaries during the language lesson?

3. When **should** young people **be allowed** to drive?
   drink?
   vote?
   go out on dates by themselves?

4. **Should** smoking **be permitted** in public places?

5. **Should** everybody (men and women) **be required** to serve in the army?

Noun/Adjective/Adverb Review:

Count/Non-Count Nouns
Comparative of Adjectives
Superlative of Adjectives
Comparative of Adverbs

many a few	much a little
paper clips eggs mushrooms · · ·	sugar paper toothpaste · · ·

Read and practice.

A. Could I possibly borrow some paper clips?*

B. Sure. **How many** do you need?

A. Just **a few**.

B. Here! Take **as many as** you want!

A. Thank you very much.

B. You're welcome.

A. Could I possibly borrow some sugar?*

B. Sure. **How much** do you need?

A. Just **a little.**

B. Here! Take **as much as** you want!

A. Thank you very much.

B. You're welcome.

*You can also say:
Could you possibly lend me some paper clips/sugar?
Could you possibly spare some paper clips/sugar?

1. *rubber bands*

2. *typing paper*

3. *eggs*

4. *shampoo*

5. *flour*

6. *envelopes*

7. *ink*

8. *mushrooms*

9. *laundry detergent*

10. *toothpaste*

11. *one-dollar bills*

12.

cheap – cheaper	interesting – more interesting
nice – nicer	beautiful – more beautiful
big – bigger	honest – more honest
friendly – friendlier	reliable – more reliable

A. I need some advice.
I can't decide whether I should **buy a used car or a new car**.
What do you think?

B. Hmm. That's a difficult question.
Used cars are **cheaper** than new cars.
On the other hand, new cars are **more reliable** than used cars.
I really don't know what to tell you.

friendly   clean   intelligent   nice

1. *buy a dog or a cat*

2. *go out on a date with Ted or Ronald*

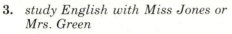

3. *study English with Miss Jones or Mrs. Green*

4. *buy ice cream or yogurt for dessert this evening*

5. *go to the supermarket across the street or the supermarket around the corner*

6. *buy a motorcycle or a bicycle*

7. *hire Mr. Clark or Mr. Davis*

8. *vote for Timothy White or Edward Pratt*

9. *take my girlfriend to a discotheque or a cafe tonight*

10.

warm	–	warmer	–	the warmest
friendly	–	friendlier	–	the friendliest
nice	–	nicer	–	the nicest
big	–	bigger	–	the biggest
interesting	–	more interesting	–	the most interesting
comfortable	–	more comfortable	–	the most comfortable
patient	–	more patient	–	the most patient

A. How do you like your new apartment?

B. I like it very much. It's really **big**.

A. Is it **bigger** than your old apartment?

B. It sure is!
It's **the biggest** apartment I've ever had.

A. How do you like your new English teacher?

B. I like him very much. He's really **patient**.

A. Is he **more patient** than your old English teacher?

B. He sure is!
He's **the most patient** English teacher I've ever had.

1. *winter coat
   warm*

2. *dance teacher
   talented*

3. *boss*
nice

4. *job*
interesting

5. *armchair*
comfortable

6. *bicycle*
fast

7. *briefcase*
sturdy

8. *vacuum cleaner*
powerful

9. *dentist*
good*

10. *roommate*
considerate

11. *parrot*
talkative

12.

*good–better–best

| gracefully – more gracefully |
| accurately – more accurately |
| carefully – more carefully |

fast – faster
well – better

A. I think I'm getting old.

B. Why do you say that?

A. I don't **dance** as **gracefully** as I used to.

B. That's not true!
You **dance more gracefully** than anybody I know.

A. You're just saying that!

B. No. I really mean it.

1. *drive*
carefully

2. *type*
accurately

3. *sing*
beautifully

4. *write*
neatly

5. *play tennis*
well

6. *jog*
fast

7. *think*
clearly

8. *work*
energetically

9. *play baseball*
well

10. *look at life*
enthusiastically

11. *speak Russian*
fluently

12.

TV COMMERCIALS

Read and practice this commercial.

A. I've been worried about my **kitchen floor** recently.

B. Really? What's the matter with your **kitchen floor**?

A. It isn't **shiny** enough, and I don't know how to make it **shinier**.
Do you have any ideas?

B. Yes, I do.
Have you ever tried PRESTO FLOOR WAX?

A. No, I haven't.
Does it make **kitchen floors shinier**?

B. It sure does!
I remember when I was worried about MY **kitchen floor**.
It wasn't as **shiny** as I wanted it to be.
But one day somebody told me about PRESTO FLOOR WAX.
I started using it, and now everybody tells me I have **the shiniest kitchen floor** in town!

A. Thanks for the advice.
I think I'll go to a store and get some right away.

B. You won't regret it.

Using the script above as a guide, prepare commercials for these products with other students in your class.

1. *windows clean*   **2.** *hair attractive*   **3.** *teeth white*   **4.**

Embedded Questions

Where is the bank?	I don't know where the bank is.
What is he doing?	I don't know what he's doing.
Why were they crying?	I don't know why they were crying.
When can he visit us?	I don't know when he can visit us.

Read and practice.

A. Where is the money?

B. I don't know where the money is.

Ask and answer these questions using one of the following expressions in your answer:

**I don't know . . ., I don't remember . . ., I can't remember . . .,
I've forgotten . . ., I'm not sure . . ., I have no idea . . .**

1. Where are my keys?

2. What was his license number?

3. What are they arguing about?

4. When will the train arrive?

5. Who should I call?

6. Who was the eleventh president of the United States?

7. How long have Mr. and Mrs. Appleton been married?

8. How long has Alan been working here?

9. When is Santa Claus going to come?

Where does he live?   I don't know where he lives.
How often do they come here?   I don't know how often they come here.
How did she break her leg?   I don't know how she broke her leg.

A. What did the robber look like?

B. I don't remember what he looked like.

I don't know . . ., I don't remember . . ., I can't remember . . .,
I've forgotten . . ., I'm not sure . . ., I have no idea . . .

1. Where did you buy your winter coat?

2. How much do eggs cost this week?

3. How often does the ice cream truck come by?

4. What time does the movie begin?

5. When did Mom and Dad get married?

6. What did we do in English class yesterday?

7. Why do young people like such loud music?

8. When did you decide to become a teacher?

9. How much does a haircut cost these days?

Where is the bank?

Do you know
Can you tell me
Could you tell me
Could you please tell me } where the bank is?
Could you possibly tell me
Do you have any idea
Do you by any chance know

What time does the concert begin?

A. Do you know what time the concert begins?

B. I'm sorry. I don't know. You should ask the man at the box office. He can tell you what time the concert begins.

How long have I been here?

A. Can you tell me how long I've been here?

B. I'm sorry. I don't know. You should ask your nurse. She can tell you how long you've been here.

When does the plane to Chicago leave?

1. *Do you know . . .*
   ask the ticket agent

Whose dog is this?

2. *Do you by any chance know . . .*
   ask the people next door

3. *Could you please tell me . . .*
ask the teacher

4. *Do you by any chance know . . .*
talk to the salesman

5. *Can you tell me . . .*
check with the mechanic

6. *Do you know . . .*
call her friend Patty

7. *Can you tell me . . .*
ask your older brother

8. *Do you know . . .*
ask that policeman over there

9. *Do you have any idea . . .*
call the superintendent

10. *Do you know . . .*
ask his supervisor

11. *Do you by any chance know . . .*
ask the boss

12.

Is Tom in school today?	Do you know $\begin{Bmatrix} \text{if} \\ \text{whether} \end{Bmatrix}$ Tom is in school today?
	I don't know $\begin{Bmatrix} \text{if} \\ \text{whether} \end{Bmatrix}$ Tom is in school today.
Does Mary work here?	Do you know $\begin{Bmatrix} \text{if} \\ \text{whether} \end{Bmatrix}$ Mary works here?
	I don't know $\begin{Bmatrix} \text{if} \\ \text{whether} \end{Bmatrix}$ Mary works here.

A. Do you know $\begin{Bmatrix} \text{if} \\ \text{whether} \end{Bmatrix}$ honey is bad for my teeth?

B. I'm not really sure. Why don't you ask your dentist?

He can tell you $\begin{Bmatrix} \text{if} \\ \text{whether} \end{Bmatrix}$ honey is bad for your teeth.

A. Can you tell me $\begin{Bmatrix} \text{if} \\ \text{whether} \end{Bmatrix}$ anybody here found a black wallet?

B. I'm not really sure. Why don't you ask the manager?

She can tell you $\begin{Bmatrix} \text{if} \\ \text{whether} \end{Bmatrix}$ anybody here found a black wallet.

1. *Can you tell me . . .*
ask the doctor

2. *Do you know . . .*
speak to the stewardess

3. *Do you know . . .*
ask Mom

4. *Could you possibly tell me . . .*
check with the ticket agent

5. *Do you by any chance know . . .*
speak to the teacher

6. *Could you please tell me . . .*
ask the bus driver

7. *Can you tell me . . .*
ask the librarian

8. *Do you know . . .*
ask the music teacher

9. *Can you tell me . . .*
check with the woman at the box office

10. *Do you know . . .*
call the landlord

11. *Can you tell me . . .*
ask those people over there

12.

I WANT TO REPORT A MISSING PERSON!

Police Department
Missing Persons Information Sheet

1. What is your name?
2. What is the missing person's name?
3. What is his/her address?
4. How old is he/she?
5. How tall is he/she?
6. How much does he/she weigh?
7. Does this person have any scars, birthmarks, or other special characteristics?
8. Where was he/she the last time you saw him/her?
9. What was he/she wearing at that time?
10. What was he/she doing?
11. What is your relationship to the missing person?
12. What is your telephone number?
13. When can we reach you at that number?

A student in your class is missing! Call the police!

I want to report a missing person!

1. Would you please tell me what your name is?

2. And would you tell me . . .

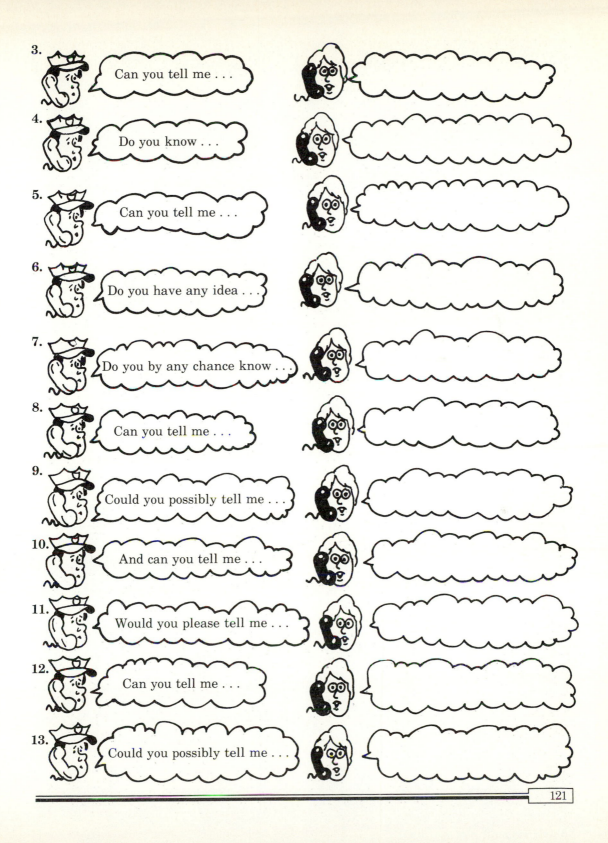

3. Can you tell me . . .

4. Do you know . . .

5. Can you tell me . . .

6. Do you have any idea . . .

7. Do you by any chance know . . .

8. Can you tell me . . .

9. Could you possibly tell me . . .

10. And can you tell me . . .

11. Would you please tell me . . .

12. Can you tell me . . .

13. Could you possibly tell me . . .

14

Perfect Modals:
Should Have
Must Have
Might Have
May Have
Could Have

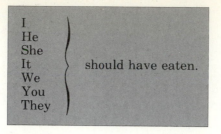

I	
He	
She	
It	should have eaten.
We	
You	
They	

Read and practice.

A. Did Richard speak loud enough in the school play last night?

B. No, he didn't.
He **should have spoken** louder.

1. Did Bob drive carefully enough during his driving test?
more carefully

2. Did Lucy study hard enough for her English exam?
harder

3. Did Theodore practice long enough for his piano lesson?
longer

4. Did Mr. and Mrs. Gleason get to the airport early enough?
earlier

5. Did Mr. Franklin write legibly enough on his income tax form?
more legibly

6. Did Harriet take her chocolate cake out of the oven soon enough?
sooner

7. Did Mr. Johnson dress comfortably enough at the beach?
more comfortably

8. Did Sally speak confidently enough at her job interview?
more confidently

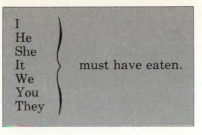

$$\left.\begin{array}{l} \text{I} \\ \text{He} \\ \text{She} \\ \text{It} \\ \text{We} \\ \text{You} \\ \text{They} \end{array}\right\} \text{must have eaten.}$$

A. Mr. Jones came to work late today.

B. I'm really surprised to hear that. Mr. Jones NEVER comes to work late!

A. I know. He **must have overslept**.

1. Sherman went to the doctor yesterday.
feel very bad

2. Beverly smoked two packs of cigarettes yesterday.
be very nervous

3. The students in my English class made lots of mistakes today.
have trouble with the lesson

4. Mr. Crabapple smiled at his employees this morning.
be in a very good mood

5. Judy refused to eat her dinner last night.
eat too many cookies after school

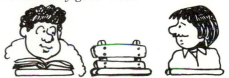

6. Maria missed English class all last week.
be very sick

7. You talked in your sleep last night.
have a bad dream

8. Walter was in a terrible mood today.
"get up on the wrong side of the bed"

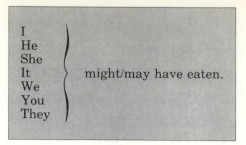

I	
He	
She	
It	} might/may have eaten.
We	
You	
They	

A. Why does John look so tired?

B. He **must have swum fifty laps** today.

A. I'm not so sure. He $\left\{ \begin{array}{c} \text{MIGHT} \\ \text{MAY} \end{array} \right\}$ **have swum fifty laps,** but **swimming fifty laps** doesn't usually make him so tired.

B. I'm a little concerned. Maybe we should talk with him.

A. That's a good idea.

A. Why does Barbara look so upset?

B. She **must have failed an exam** today.

A. I'm not so sure. She $\left\{ \begin{array}{c} \text{MIGHT} \\ \text{MAY} \end{array} \right\}$ **have failed an exam,** but **failing an exam** doesn't usually make her so upset.

B. I'm a little concerned. Maybe we should talk with her.

A. That's a good idea.

1. Why does Martha look so nervous?
drink* too much coffee

2. Why does Fred look so tired?
work overtime

3. Why does Peggy look so exhausted?
jog a little too much

4. Why does Peter look so upset?
argue with the boss

5. Why does Senator Johnson look so tired?
shake† a lot of hands

6. Why does Roger look so upset?
have a fight with his girlfriend

7. Why does our English teacher look so angry?
find a lot of mistakes in our homework

8. Why does our cat look so scared?
be chased by the dog across the street

*drink–drank–drunk
†shake–shook–shaken

| I He She It We You They | } could have eaten. |

A. You won't believe what George did yesterday!

B. What did he do?

A. He moved his piano by himself.

B. You're kidding!
He shouldn't have moved his piano by himself.

A. Of course he shouldn't have. He {**could** / **might**} **have broken his back!**

1. *go hiking by himself in the mountains*
get lost

2. *eat all the ice cream in the refrigerator*
get sick

3. *go skating on the town pond*
fall* through the ice

4. *play baseball in the rain*
catch a bad cold

*fall–fell–fallen

5. *ride her bicycle downtown*
get hurt

6. *swim to the other side of the lake*
drown

7. *try to fix their TV by themselves*
be electrocuted

8. *shout back at the boss*
get fired

9. *run in the Boston Marathon*
have a heart attack

10. *mix nitric acid and glycerin*
blow* up the school

11. *get into an argument with*
a policeman
wind up in jail

12.

*blow–blew–blown

Read and practice.

I OWE YOU AN APOLOGY

A. I owe you an apology.

B. What for?

A. You must have been very angry with me yesterday.

B. I don't understand. Why should I have been angry with you?

A. Don't you remember?
We had planned to **see a movie** yesterday, but I completely forgot!

B. Don't worry about it.
In fact, I owe YOU an apology.

A. You do? Why?

B. I couldn't have **seen a movie** with you anyway. I had to **take care of my little sister** yesterday . . . and I completely forgot to tell you.

A. That's O.K. Maybe we can **see a movie** some time soon.

A. I owe you an apology.

B. What for?

A. You must have been very angry with me yesterday.

B. I don't understand. Why should I have been angry with you?

A. Don't you remember?
We had planned to _____ yesterday, but I completely forgot!

B. Don't worry about it.
In fact, I owe YOU an apology.

A. You do? Why?

B. I couldn't have _____ with you anyway.
I had to _____ yesterday . . . and I completely forgot to tell you.

A. That's O.K. Maybe we can _____ some time soon.

1. *play tennis*
go to the doctor

2. *go swimming*
visit a friend in the hospital

3. *have lunch*
go to an important meeting

4.

15

Conditional:
Present Real
(If _____ Will)
Present Unreal
(If _____ Would)
Hope-Clauses

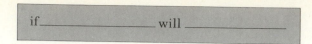

if _____ will _____

Read and practice.

A. What are you going to do this weekend?

B. We aren't sure.
If the weather is good, we'll probably go to the beach.
If the weather is bad, we'll probably stay home.

1. How is Tom going to get to work tomorrow?

He isn't sure.
If it rains, _____.
If it's sunny, _____.

2. What are Mr. and Mrs. Green going to do tonight?

They aren't sure.
If they're tired, _____.
If they have some energy, _____.

3. Where are you going to have lunch today?

I'm not sure.
If I'm in a hurry, _____.
If I have some time, _____.

4. What's Jane going to do tomorrow?

She isn't sure.
If she still has a cold, _____.
If she feels better, _____.

5. Where is Patty going to go after school today?

She isn't sure.
If she has a lot of homework, _____.
If she doesn't have a lot of homework, _____.

6. What's Henry going to have for dessert this evening?

He isn't sure.
If he decides to stay on his diet, _____.
If he decides to forget about his diet, _____.

A. Do you think Johnny should go to school today?

B. No, I don't.
If Johnny goes to school today, he might **give his cold to the other children**.

1. Do you think I should put some
   more salt in the soup?
   spoil it

2. Do you think I should skip
   English class today?
   miss something important

3. Do you think Rover should come
   to the beach with us?
   get carsick

4. Do you think I should try to
   break up that fight?
   get hurt

5. Do you think Mary should quit
   her job?
   have trouble finding another one

6. Do you think Teddy should stay up
   and watch TV with us?
   have trouble getting up in the morning

7. Do you think I should marry Norman?
   regret it for the rest of your life

8.

I hope it rains tomorrow.
I hope it doesn't rain tomorrow.

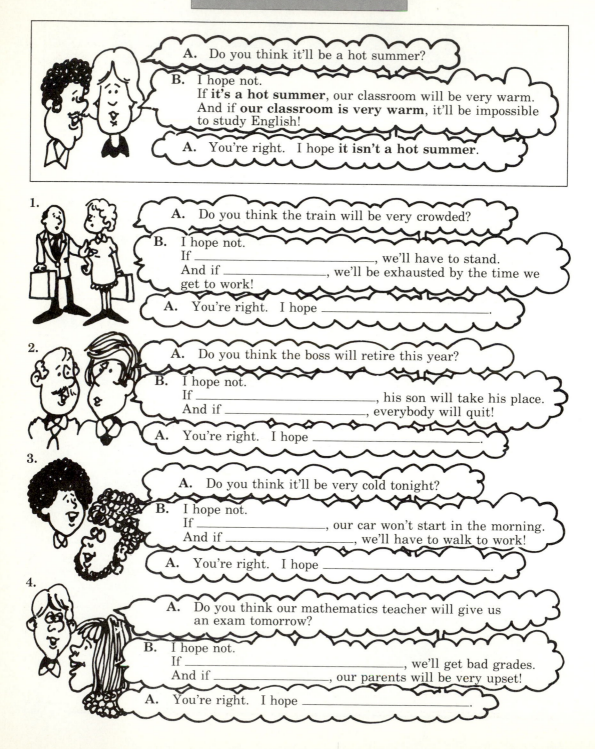

A. Do you think it'll be a hot summer?

B. I hope not.
If **it's a hot summer**, our classroom will be very warm.
And if **our classroom is very warm**, it'll be impossible to study English!

A. You're right. I hope **it isn't a hot summer**.

1.

A. Do you think the train will be very crowded?

B. I hope not.
If _____, we'll have to stand.
And if _____, we'll be exhausted by the time we get to work!

A. You're right. I hope _____.

2.

A. Do you think the boss will retire this year?

B. I hope not.
If _____, his son will take his place.
And if _____, everybody will quit!

A. You're right. I hope _____.

3.

A. Do you think it'll be very cold tonight?

B. I hope not.
If _____, our car won't start in the morning.
And if _____, we'll have to walk to work!

A. You're right. I hope _____.

4.

A. Do you think our mathematics teacher will give us an exam tomorrow?

B. I hope not.
If _____, we'll get bad grades.
And if _____, our parents will be very upset!

A. You're right. I hope _____.

5.

A. Do you think it'll rain tomorrow?

B. I hope not.
If _____, we'll have to cancel the school picnic.
And if _____, everybody will be very disappointed!

A. You're right. I hope _____.

6.

A. Do you think the bus will be late today?

B. I hope not.
If _____, we won't get to work on time.
And if _____, the boss will be very angry!

A. You're right. I hope _____.

7.

A. Do you think inflation will get worse this year?

B. I hope not.
If _____, I'll have to take a second job.
And if _____, my family will be very upset!

A. You're right. I hope _____.

8.

A. Do you think our landlord will raise the rent this year?

B. I hope not.
If _____, we won't be able to pay it.
And if _____, we'll have to move!

A. You're right. I hope _____.

9.

A. Do you think our TV will be at the repair shop for a long time?

B. I hope not.
If _____, we won't have anything to do in the evening.
And if _____, we'll go crazy!

A. You're right. I hope _____.

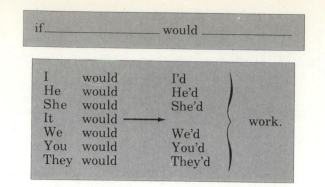

I	would		I'd	
He	would		He'd	
She	would		She'd	
It	would	→		work.
We	would		We'd	
You	would		You'd	
They	would		They'd	

A. Why don't our grandchildren visit us more often?

B. They don't have enough time.
   If they had more time, they'd visit us more often.

A. Why isn't Melvin a good salesman?

B. He isn't aggressive enough.
   If he were* more aggressive, he'd be a good salesman.

*If [I, he, she, it, we, you, they] were . . .

1. A. Why doesn't Sally get good grades?
   B. She doesn't study enough.
   If_____.

2. A. Why isn't Mark a good driver?
   B. He isn't careful enough.
   If_____.

3.
A. Why don't I feel energetic?
B. You don't sleep enough.
If_____.

4.
A. Why doesn't Alexander enjoy playing baseball?
B. He isn't athletic enough.
If_____.

5.
A. Why doesn't Julie have friends at school?
B. She isn't outgoing enough.
If_____.

6.
A. Why doesn't Sidney have a yearly checkup?
B. He isn't concerned enough about his health.
If_____.

7.
A. Why aren't you satisfied with your jobs?
B. We don't get paid enough.
If_____.

8.
A. Why don't I enjoy life?
B. You aren't relaxed enough.
If_____.

9.
A. Why aren't most Americans in good physical condition?
B. They don't exercise enough.
If_____.

10.
A. Why don't Tom and Janet get along with each other?
B. They don't have enough in common.
If_____.

11.
A. Why don't our congressmen do something about pollution?
B. They aren't concerned enough about the environment.
If_____.

12.
A. Why doesn't our English teacher buy a new pair of shoes?
B. He doesn't make enough money.
If_____.

A. I wonder why Fred works so hard.

B. I don't know. He must like his job.

A. You're probably right.
If he didn't like his job, he wouldn't work so hard.

A. I wonder why my older brother and his girlfriend hold hands all the time.

B. I don't know. They must be in love.

A. You're probably right.
If they weren't in love, they wouldn't hold hands all the time.

1. I wonder why Barbara wants to be a schoolteacher.
She must like children.

2. I wonder why Alan makes so many mistakes.
He must be careless.

3. I wonder why Nancy is so nervous.
She must have an exam today.

4. I wonder why our teacher is shouting at us today.
She must be in a bad mood.

5. I wonder why Rover is barking at the door.
He must want to go outside.

6. I wonder why Bob is so dressed up today.
He must be going to a job interview.

7. I wonder why John gets into so many fights.
He must like to argue with people.

8. I wonder why Judy wants a telescope for her birthday.
She must be interested in astronomy.

9. I wonder why Jeff is home tonight.
He must have to take care of his little brother.

10. I wonder why Shirley goes hiking in the mountains every weekend.
She must enjoy nature.

11. I wonder why I'm sneezing so much.
You must be allergic to my perfume.

12.

ARE YOU PREPARED FOR EMERGENCIES?

Answer these questions and ask other students in your class.

1. What would you do if you saw someone choking on a piece of food?

2. What would you do if you saw someone having a heart attack?

3. What would you do if you were at the beach and you saw someone drowning?

4. What would you do if somebody in your family were missing?

5. What would you do if somebody came up to you on the street and tried to rob you?

6. What would you do if a fire broke out in your house or apartment?

7. What would you do if you were lying in bed and you heard someone trying to break into your house or apartment?

8. What would you do if you were bitten by a dog?

Think of some other emergencies and ask other students if they're prepared:

_____

_____

_____

Present Unreal Conditional (continued)
Wish-Clauses

Read and practice.

A. Do you think the boss would be angry if I went home early?

B. Of course he would. He'd be VERY angry.

A. Do you really think so?

B. I'm positive.*
I wouldn't go home early if I were you.

A. I suppose you're right.

*You can also say: Without a doubt.   There's no question in my mind.

1. Do you think Roger would be disappointed if I missed his birthday party?

2. Do you think our English teacher would be upset if I skipped class tomorrow?

3. Do you think Mom and Dad would be angry if I borrowed the car?

4. Do you think our neighbors would be annoyed if I turned on the stereo?

5. Do you think Jack would be jealous if I took out his girlfriend?

6. Do you think the voters would be upset if I raised taxes?

7. Do you think Jennifer would be mad if I rode her bicycle?

8. Do you think the landlord would be upset if I painted the kitchen purple?

9. Do you think my parents would be disappointed if I dropped out of school?

10. Do you think my fans would be unhappy if I got a haircut?

11. Do you think Tom would be embarrassed if I showed his girlfriend a photograph of him in the bathtub when he was two years old?

12.

Tom **lives** in Boston.   He **wishes** he **lived** in New York.

A. Do you enjoy driving a school bus?

B. Not really.
I wish I drove a taxi.

A. Does Mr. Robinson enjoy being a teacher?

B. Not really.
He wishes he were an actor.

1. Does Mary enjoy living in the suburbs?
in the city

2. Does Mrs. Kramer enjoy teaching math?
something else

3. Does Larry enjoy being single?
married

4. Do you enjoy working here?
someplace else

5. Does Ralph enjoy selling used cars?
insurance

6. Does Oscar enjoy painting houses?
portraits

7. Do you enjoy being the vice-president?
the president

8. Does Sarah enjoy having two part-time jobs?
one good full-time job

9.

Mary can sing.   She wishes she could dance.

A. Can Jonathan dance?

B. No, he can't . . . but he wishes he could.
If he could dance, he'd **go dancing every night**.

1. Can Mary sew?
make all her own clothes

2. Can Steve quit smoking?
be a lot healthier

3. Can Gloria find her keys?
be able to get into her apartment

4. Can Richard find his glasses?
watch TV tonight

5. Can Janet type fast?
be able to get a better job

6. Can Henry fix his car by himself?
save a lot of money

7. Can Maria stop thinking about
tomorrow's English test?
get a good night's sleep

8. Can Ronald play a musical
instrument?
*be able to march
in the school parade*

9. Can Jessica talk?
*tell her parents she doesn't like
her baby food*

10.

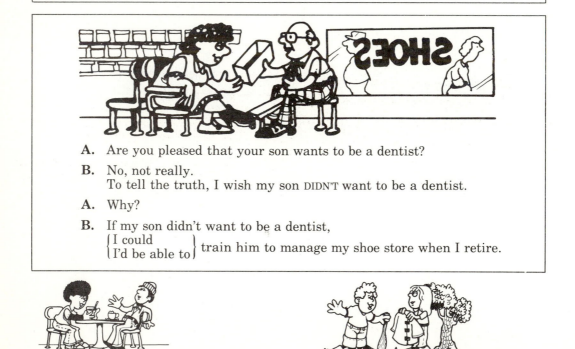

A. Are you glad that your landlord is going to repaint your apartment this Saturday?

B. No, not really.
To tell the truth, I wish my landlord WEREN'T going to repaint my apartment this Saturday.

A. Why?

B. If my landlord weren't going to repaint my apartment this Saturday, {I could / I'd be able to} go away for the weekend.

A. Are you pleased that your son wants to be a dentist?

B. No, not really.
To tell the truth, I wish my son DIDN'T want to be a dentist.

A. Why?

B. If my son didn't want to be a dentist, {I could / I'd be able to} train him to manage my shoe store when I retire.

---

1. Are you happy that your aunt and uncle are coming to visit tomorrow?
go skiing

2. Are you glad that the weather is going to be nice this weekend?
wear my new raincoat for the first time

3. Are you happy that the boss wants to take you to dinner tomorrow?
go home early

4. Are you glad that the TV is fixed?
talk to the children

5. Are you happy that your daughter is going to a college out of town?
see her more often

6. Are you glad that you live in a high-rise building?
have a garden

7. Are you pleased that your son takes drum lessons?
have some "peace and quiet" around the house

8. Are you happy that your parents are going to have a birthday party for you this Saturday?
go out and celebrate with my friends

9. Are you pleased that your new office has a view of the park?
concentrate more on my work

10. Are you glad that you're studying difficult grammar now?
do my homework in just a few minutes

I NEED SOME ADVICE

Read and practice.

A. Would you mind if I asked you for some advice?

B. Of course I wouldn't mind.

A. I'm thinking of **buying a used car from Ralph Jones**, but I'm not sure that's a very good idea.   What do you think?

B. Do you want my honest opinion?

A. Yes, of course.

B. Well . . . to tell the truth, I wouldn't **buy a used car from Ralph Jones** if I were you.   If you **bought a used car from Ralph Jones**, you'd probably **regret it**.

A. I guess you're right.   Thanks for the advice.

1. *ask the boss for a raise this week*
get fired

2. *grow a moustache*
look very funny

3. *work overtime this weekend*
be exhausted by Monday morning

4.

Past Unreal Conditional
(If ____ Would Have ____)
Wish-Clauses (continued)

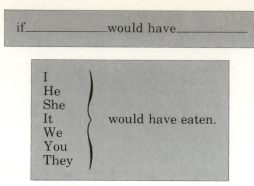

if_____would have_____

I	
He	
She	
It	would have eaten.
We	
You	
They	

Read and practice.

A. Why didn't Peter take his umbrella to work today?

B. He didn't know it was going to rain.
If he had known it was going to rain, he would have taken his umbrella to work today.

EXERCISE CLASS

A. Why weren't you in class yesterday?

B. I wasn't feeling well.
If I had been feeling well, I would have been in class yesterday.

1. A. Why didn't you do your homework last night?

B. I didn't bring my book home.
If_____.

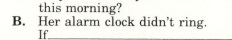

2. A. Why wasn't Sally on time for work this morning?

B. Her alarm clock didn't ring.
If_____.

3. A. Why didn't you send me a postcard?
B. We didn't remember your address.
If_____.

4. A. Why didn't Mr. and Mrs. Clark watch the President's speech last night?
B. Their TV wasn't working.
If_____.

5. A. Why didn't you come * to the party last night?
B. I wasn't invited.
If_____.

6. A. Why didn't Mrs. Brown's students give her a birthday present?
B. She didn't tell them it was her birthday.
If_____.

7. A. Why didn't you make your beds this morning?
B. We didn't have enough time.
If_____.

8. A. Why didn't you go to the movies with your friends last night?
B. I wasn't in the mood to see a film.
If_____.

9. A. Why didn't Mr. and Mrs. Green enjoy the play last night?
B. They didn't have good seats.
If_____.

10. A. Why wasn't Senator Maxwell re-elected?
B. The people didn't trust him.
If_____.

11. A. Why didn't Harry stop at that traffic light?
B. He wasn't looking.
If_____.

12. A. Why wasn't Sophia asked to sing an encore last night?
B. The audience wasn't pleased with her performance.
If_____.

*come–came–come

A. I wonder why John ran by without saying hello.

B. He must have **been in a hurry**.

A. You're probably right.
If he hadn't been in a hurry, he wouldn't have run by without saying hello.

1. I wonder why Gregory arrived late for work.
miss the bus

2. I wonder why Mario was absent from English class all last week.
be very sick

3. I wonder why Betty quit.
find a better job

4. I wonder why Rover got sick last night.
eat something he shouldn't have

5. I wonder why the apple pie tasted so fresh.
be baked this morning

6. I wonder why Mom went to sleep so early.
have a hard day at the office

7. I wonder why Helen prepared so much food.
expect a lot of people to come to her party

8. I wonder why the boss was so irritable today.
be upset about something

9. I wonder why my cactus plant died.
have a rare disease

10. I wonder why Eleanor went home early today.
be feeling "under the weather"

11. I wonder why Dad got stopped by a policeman.
be driving too fast

12. I wonder why my barber cut my hair so quickly today.
have a lot of customers after you

13. I wonder why my shirt shrank* so much.
be 100 percent cotton

14.

*shrink–shrank–shrunk

Tom **lives** in Boston. He **wishes** he **lived** in New York.	Tom **lived** in Boston. He **wishes** he **had lived** in New York.

A. Does Albert know his neighbors?

B. No, he doesn't.
But he WISHES he **knew his neighbors**.
If he knew his neighbors, he wouldn't **be so lonely**.

A. Did Linda know how to get around the city when she moved here?

B. No, she didn't.
But she WISHES she **had known how to get around the city.**
If she had known how to get around the city, she wouldn't have **been so confused.**

1. Does Donald have a good memory?
forget people's names all the time

2. Did Sharon have her shopping list with her this morning?
forget* to buy eggs

***forget–forgot–forgotten**

3. Does Judy drive to work?
have to wait for the bus every morning

4. Did you drive to work today?
have to wait forty minutes for the subway

5. Does Paul have a good job?
be so concerned about his future

6. Did you have a flu shot last fall?
be sick all winter

7. Does Brenda do daily exercises?
have to go on a diet

8. Did Ivan do his homework last night?
have to do his homework early this morning

9. Is Philip an optimist?
get depressed so often

10. Was Alice prepared for her English test?
get a low grade

11. Do Mr. and Mrs. Taylor take dance lessons?
feel so "out of place" at discotheques

12. Did Harry take two aspirin when his tooth began to hurt?
feel so much pain

WISHES AND HOPES

I hope it's sunny tomorrow.   (It might be sunny.)
I wish it were sunny.   (It isn't sunny.)
I wish it had been sunny   (It wasn't sunny.)
  during our picnic.

Read and practice.

1.

A. I hope it's a nice day tomorrow.

B. How come?

A. If it's a nice day tomorrow, we'll be able to go to the beach.

2.

A. I wish I were taller.

B. Why?

A. If I were taller, I'd be able to reach the cookie jar.

3.

A. I wish I had saved my wedding dress.

B. Why?

A. If I had saved my wedding dress, I could have given it to you for your wedding.

4.

A. I wish I had finished medical school.

B. What makes you say that?

A. If I had finished medical school, I probably would have been a very good doctor.

5.

A. I hope we don't have to go to school tomorrow.

B. I hope so, too.

A. If we don't have to go to school tomorrow, we can play outside all day and build a snowman.

6.

A. I wish I didn't have to go to work tomorrow.

B. Why?

A. If I didn't have to go to work tomorrow, I could watch my daughter perform in her school play.

7.

A. I wish we hadn't bought Teddy a chemistry set for his birthday.

B. How come?

A. If we hadn't bought Teddy a chemistry set for his birthday, he wouldn't have set the house on fire.

What do YOU hope? What do YOU wish? Why?
Share your thoughts with other students in your class.

Reported Speech
Sequence of Tenses

He said,	He said (that)*
"I'm sick."	. . . he was sick.
"I like jazz."	. . . he liked jazz.
"I'm going to buy a new car."	. . . he was going to buy a new car.
"I went to Paris last year."	. . . he had gone to Paris last year.
"I've already seen that movie."	. . . he had already seen that movie.
"I was studying."	. . . he had been studying.
"I'll call you tomorrow."	. . . he would call me tomorrow.
"I can help you."	. . . he could help me.

Read and practice.

A. I forgot to tell you. Marvin called yesterday.

B. Really? What did he say?

A. He said (that)* **he thought he was falling in love with me**.

A. I forgot to tell you. _____ called yesterday.

B. Really? What did _____ say?

A. _____ said (that)*_____.

*You can also say: told me (that).

1.

"I'm working very hard at college this year."

our oldest son

2.

"I can't fix your TV."

the TV repairman

3.

"I got a raise last week."

our niece Patty

4.

"I've been fired."

our nephew Robert

5.

"I'll be arriving this Friday on the two o'clock train."

Uncle Charlie

6.

"We're going to move to a new apartment."

our upstairs neighbors

7.

"You don't have to work overtime next week."

my boss

8.

"We won't be able to come to your party."

Peggy and George

9.

"I'll send you a postcard from Rome."

Aunt Edith

10.

"I'm sorry I forgot about your birthday."

my boyfriend

11.

"I'll be glad to baby-sit this Saturday night."

the little girl down the street

12.

"The car is ready and you can pick it up any time you want to."

the auto mechanic

13.

"I saw you at the shopping mall, but you didn't see me."

my sister

14.

"I was planning to visit this weekend, but I won't be able to come because I have the flu."

Grandma

John works here.	I knew I didn't know } (that) John worked here.

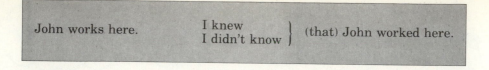

A. What's everybody talking about?

B. Haven't you heard?
Jack is going to be a father!

A. You're kidding! I didn't know (that) Jack was going to be a father.

B. You didn't?! I thought EVERYBODY knew (that) Jack was going to be a father!

A. What's everybody_____ about?

B. Haven't you heard?
_____!

A. You're kidding! I didn't know (that)_____.

B. You didn't?! I thought EVERYBODY knew (that)_____!

1. What's everybody so upset about?

2. What's everybody talking about?

3. What's everybody so happy about?

4. What's everybody so upset about?

5. What's everybody so angry about?

6. What's everybody so nervous about?

7. What's everybody so excited about?

8. What's everybody so happy about?

9. What's everybody so excited about?

10. What's everybody talking about?

11. What's everybody so upset about?

12.

He asked,	He asked me
"Where is the bank?"	. . . where the bank was.
"When are you going to visit me?"	. . . when I was going to visit him.
"Do you speak English?"	. . . $\begin{Bmatrix} \text{if} \\ \text{whether} \end{Bmatrix}$ I spoke English.
"Have you seen Mary?"	. . . $\begin{Bmatrix} \text{if} \\ \text{whether} \end{Bmatrix}$ I had seen Mary.

A. You won't believe what a three-year-old girl asked me today!

B. What did she ask you?

A. She asked me why there was a Santa Claus in every department store in town.

B. I can't believe she asked you that!

A. I can't either.

A. You won't believe what a taxi driver asked me today!

B. What did he ask you?

A. He asked me $\begin{Bmatrix} \text{if} \\ \text{whether} \end{Bmatrix}$ I knew how to fix a flat tire.

B. I can't believe he asked you that!

A. I can't either.

A. You won't believe what _____ asked me today!

B. What did ____ ask you?

A. ____ asked me _____.

B. I can't believe _____ asked you that!

A. I can't either.

1. *my math teacher*

2. *my boyfriend*

3. *my employees*

4. *my students*

5. *the woman at my job interview*

6. *my philosophy professor*

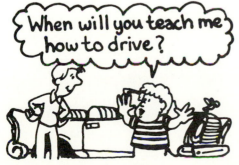

7. *my nine-year-old nephew*

8. *my basketball coach*

9. *our downstairs neighbors*

10. *my daughter*

11. *my parents*

12. *my boss*

13. *my son*

14. *one of my patients*

15. *a door-to-door salesman*

16.

He said,	He told me
"Call me after five o'clock."	. . . to call him after five o'clock.
"Stop smoking!"	. . . to stop smoking.
"Don't worry!"	. . . not to worry.
"Don't call me before nine o'clock."	. . . not to call him before nine o'clock.

A. I'm a little annoyed at the mailman.

B. How come?

A. He told me to keep my dog in the house.

B. Why did he tell you that?

A. He said (that) he was afraid to deliver my mail.

A. I'm a little annoyed at my English students.

B. How come?

A. They told me not to give them any homework this weekend.

B. Why did they tell you that?

A. They said (that) they were tired of English grammar.

A. I'm a little annoyed at _____.

B. How come?

A. ____ told me _____.

B. Why did _____ tell you that?

A. _____ said (that) _____.

1. *my doctor*

2. *my girlfriend*

3. *the school-bus driver*

4. *my dentist*

5. *my neighbors across the hall*

6. *my teacher*

7. *my nurse*

8. *my boss*

9. *my parents*

10. *my seven-year-old son*

11. *my landlord*

12. *my neighbors across the street*

ON YOUR OWN

1. Do you remember the last time somebody said something that really annoyed you?

What did the person say?
(He/She told me . . .)
Why do you think he/she said that?
Did you say anything back?

Talk about this with other students in your class.

2. "Bob would be angry if somebody told him he didn't play baseball very well."
"Patty would be upset if her parents told her to stop watching TV."
"Mike would be jealous if his girlfriend told him she wanted to go out with other boys."

Do you get angry, upset or jealous very easily? Complete these sentences and discuss with other students in your class:

1. I would be angry if _____ told me _____.
2. I would be upset if _____ told me _____.
3. I would be jealous if _____ told me _____.

Tag Questions
Emphatic Sentences

John **is** here, **isn't** he?	Yes, he **is**.	No, he **isn't**.
You **were** sick, **weren't** you?	Yes, I **was**.	No, I **wasn't**.
Maria **will** be here soon, **won't** she?	Yes, she **will**.	No, she **won't**.
Bobby **has** gone to bed, **hasn't** he?	Yes, he **has**.	No, he **hasn't**.
You like ice cream, **don't** you?	Yes, I **do**.	No, I **don't**.
Henry worked yesterday, **didn't** he?	Yes, he **did**.	No, he **didn't**.

Read and practice.

A. The bus stops at this corner, doesn't it?

B. Yes, it does.

A. That's what I thought.

1. You live in apartment seventeen, _____?

2. I can smoke here, _____?

3. Abraham Lincoln was our sixteenth president, _____?

4. You locked the front door, _____?

5. The President is going to speak on TV tonight, _____?

6. Miss Smith will be out of town next week, _____?

7. We've already seen this movie, _____?

8. You were a waiter in the restaurant across the street, _____?

9. You're a famous movie star, _____?

174

John **isn't** here, **is** he?	Yes, he **is**.	No, he **isn't**.
You **weren't** angry, **were** you?	Yes, I **was**.	No, I **wasn't**.
Sally **won't** be late, **will** she?	Yes, she **will**.	No, she **won't**.
You **haven't** eaten, **have** you?	Yes, I **have**.	No, I **haven't**.
George **doesn't** smoke, **does** he?	Yes, he **does**.	No, he **doesn't**.
They **didn't** leave, **did** they?	Yes, they **did**.	No, they **didn't**.

A. Your son isn't allergic to penicillin, is he?

B. No, he isn't.

A. That's what I thought.

1. The children don't ride this old bicycle any more, _____?

2. We didn't have any homework for today, _____?

3. I can't have any more candy, _____?

4. You aren't really going to go swimming today, _____?

5. The mail hasn't come yet, _____?

6. There weren't any airplanes when you were a little boy, _____?

7. Dr. Anderson won't be in the office tomorrow, _____?

8. I shouldn't take these pills right after I eat, _____?

9. I haven't taught "tag questions" before, _____?

A. You like to dance, don't you?

B. No, I don't.

A. You DON'T?! I'm really surprised!
I was SURE you liked to dance!

A. This park isn't dangerous at night, is it?

B. Yes, it is.

A. It IS?! I'm really surprised!
I was SURE this park wasn't dangerous at night!

1. A. It's going to be a nice day tomorrow, _____?

B. No, _____.

2. A. The children aren't asleep yet, _____?

B. Yes, _____.

3. A. This building has an elevator, _____?

B. No, _____.

4. A. I don't have to wear a tie in this restaurant, _____?

B. Yes, _____.

5. A. The post office hasn't closed yet, _____?

B. Yes, _____.

6. A. You can swim, _____?

B. No, _____.

7. A. I did well on the exam, _____?

B. No, _____.

8. A. Dolphins can't talk, _____?

B. Yes, _____.

9. A. The earth is flat, _____?

B. No, _____.

10. A. I wasn't going over fifty-five miles per hour, _____?

B. Yes, _____.

11. A. We have a spare tire, _____?

B. No, _____.

12. A. You won't be offended if I don't finish your delicious cake, _____?

B. Yes, _____.

CONGRATULATIONS!

A. I have some good news!

B. What is it?

A. My wife and I are celebrating our fiftieth wedding anniversary tomorrow!

B. You ARE?!

A. Yes, we are.

B. I don't believe it! You aren't REALLY celebrating your fiftieth wedding anniversary tomorrow, are you?

A. Yes, it's true. We ARE!

B. Well, congratulations! I'm very glad to hear that!

A. I have some good news!

B. What is it?

A. I got a fifty-dollar-a-week raise!

B. You DID?!

A. Yes, I did.

B. I don't believe it! You didn't REALLY get a fifty-dollar-a-week raise, did you?

A. Yes, it's true. I DID!

B. Well, congratulations! I'm very glad to hear that!

1. I won the lottery!

2. I'm going to have a baby!

3. I've been promoted!

4. The mayor wants me to paint his portrait!

5. I'm going to be the star of the school play!

6. We've found the man who robbed your house!

7. I can tie my shoes by myself!

8. My daughter has been accepted to Harvard University!

9. We won the football championship today!

10. I was interviewed by *The New York Times* yesterday!

11. I've discovered the cure for the common cold!

12.

Mary is late.
George was angry.
They aren't very friendly.
I don't know the answer.

They work hard.
John looks tired.
Janet came late to class.

Mary IS late.
George WAS angry.
They AREN'T very friendly.
I DON'T know the answer.

They DO work hard.
John DOES look tired.
Janet DID come late to class.

A. You know . . . the color blue looks very good on you.

B. Come to think of it, you're right!
The color blue DOES look very good on me, doesn't it.

A. You know . . . it isn't a very good day to fly a kite.

B. Come to think of it, you're right!
It ISN'T a very good day to fly a kite, is it.

1. . . . you work too hard.

2. . . . Rover is a very talented dog.

3. . . . Uncle Frank hasn't called in a long time.

4. . . . that was an awful movie.

5. . . . this milk tastes sour.

6. . . . you have quite a few gray hairs.

7. . . . we really shouldn't be hitchhiking at night.

8. . . . Lesson 19 is easier than Lesson 18.

9. . . . little Bobby talks in much longer sentences now.

10. . . . you won't be able to play soccer for several months.

11. . . . you've been talking on the telephone for a long time.

12. . . . our English teacher gave us a lot of homework last night.

13. . . . our grandchildren don't write as often as they used to.

14. . . . the choir sang beautifully this morning.

15. . . . your brother Peter and my sister Margaret would probably make a nice couple.

16. . . . you did your homework very carelessly.

17. . . . this new toaster doesn't work very well.

18.

Read and practice.

A. You're tired, aren't you.

B. Tired? What makes you think I'm tired?

A. Well, you're falling asleep at the wheel.

B. Now that you mention it, I guess I AM falling asleep at the wheel, aren't I.*

A. You're nervous, aren't you.

B. Nervous? What makes you think I'm nervous?

A. Well, you haven't stopped smoking since early this morning.

B. Now that you mention it, I guess I HAVEN'T stopped smoking since early this morning, have I.

---

*

He's			We're			
She's	late, isn't	he. she.	You're	late, aren't	we. you.	I'm late, **aren't** I.
It's		it	They're		they	

A. You're in a bad mood, aren't you.

B. In a bad mood? What makes you think I'm in a bad mood?

A. Well, you shouted at me a few minutes ago.

B. Now that you mention it, I guess I DID shout at you a few minutes ago, didn't I.

A. You're_____, aren't you.

B. _____? What makes you think I'm_____?

A. Well,_____.

B. Now that you mention it, I guess_____, _____ _____.

Complete these conversations and try them with other students in your class.

1. *nervous*

2. *angry*

3. *upset*

4. *bored*

5. *embarrassed*

6. *jealous*

Review:
Verb Tenses
Conditionals
Gerunds

Read and practice.

A. Would you like to **go on a picnic** with me today?

B. I don't think so.   To be honest, I really don't feel like **going on a picnic** today. I **went on a picnic** yesterday.

A. That's too bad.   I'm really disappointed.

B. I hope you understand.
If I hadn't **gone on a picnic** yesterday, I'd be VERY happy to **go on a picnic** with you today.

A. OF COURSE I understand!
After all, I suppose you'd get tired of **going on picnics** if you **went on picnics** all the time!

A. Would you like to _____ with me today?

B. I don't think so.   To be honest, I really don't feel like _____ing today.
I _____ yesterday.

A. That's too bad.   I'm really disappointed.

B. I hope you understand.
If I hadn't _____ yesterday, I'd be VERY happy to
_____ with you today.

A. OF COURSE I understand!
After all, I suppose you'd get tired of _____ing if you _____
all the time!

1. *swim*

2. *see a movie*

3. *go dancing*

4. *play chess*

5. *eat at a restaurant*

6. *drive around town*

7. *study Algebra*

8. *go shopping*

9. *take a walk in the park*

10.

A. Do you realize what you just did?

B. No. What did I just do?

A. You just **ate both our salads**!

B. I did?

A. Yes. You did.

B. I'm really sorry. I must have **been very hungry**.
If I hadn't **been very hungry**, I NEVER would have **eaten both our salads!**

1. *drive past my house*
forget your address

2. *step on my feet*
lose my balance

3. *go through a red light*
be daydreaming

4. *hit me with your umbrella*
be looking the other way

5. *paint the living room window*
have my mind on something else

6. *call me Gloria*
be thinking about somebody else

7. *drink all the milk in the refrigerator*
be really thirsty

8. *throw out my homework*
think it was scrap paper

9. *put my pen in your pocket*
think it was mine

10. *put tomatoes in the onion soup*
misunderstand the recipe

11. *give Mr. Smith's medicine to Mr. Jones*
mix up Mr. Jones and Mr. Smith

12. *sit on my cat*
think it was a pillow

A. You seem upset. Is anything wrong?

B. Yes. **The heating system in my building is broken.**

A. I'm sorry to hear that.
How long **has it been broken?**

B. **It's been broken** for **two days**.

A. I know how upset you must be.
I remember when **the heating system in MY building was broken**.
Is there anything I can do to help?

B. Not really. But thanks for your concern.

A. You seem upset. Is anything wrong?

B. Yes. _____.

A. I'm sorry to hear that.
How long _____?

B. _____ (for/since) _____.

A. I know how upset you must be.
I remember when _____.
Is there anything I can do to help?

B. Not really. But thanks for your concern.

1. My best friend is angry at me.

2. My father is in the hospital.

3. My TV is broken.

4. My girlfriend wants to break up with me.

5. I'm unemployed.*

6. The elevator in my apartment building is out of order.

7. I'm having trouble sleeping at night.

8. My landlord refuses to fix my bathtub.

9. My dog is lost.

10. My wisdom teeth hurt.

11. I have cockroaches in my apartment.

12. I'm having trouble communicating with my teenage daughter.

*You can also say: I'm out of work.

A. Hello, Bob. This is Sam.

B. Hi, Sam. How are you?

A. I'm O.K.
Listen, Bob . . . I'm trying to **put in my air-conditioner**, but I'm having trouble **putting it in** by myself. Could you possibly come over and give me a hand?

B. I'm really sorry, Sam. I'm afraid I can't come over right now.
My relatives are visiting from Chicago.
If **my relatives weren't visiting from Chicago**, I'd be GLAD to help you **put your air-conditioner in**.

A. Don't worry about it.
If I had known **your relatives were visiting from Chicago,**
I wouldn't have even called you in the first place!

A. Hello, _____. This is _____.

B. Hi, _____. How are you?

A. I'm O.K.
Listen, _____ . . . I'm trying to _____, but I'm having trouble _____ing by myself. Could you possibly come over and give me a hand?

B. I'm really sorry, _____. I'm afraid I can't come over right now.
_____.
If _____, I'd be GLAD to help you _____.

A. Don't worry about it.
If I had known _____,
I wouldn't have even called you in the first place!

1. *hang up a portrait of*
   my grandfather
   "I'm late for a job interview."

2. *fix my stove*
   "I have a bad cold."

3. *move my piano*
   "I have to wait for the plumber."

4. *figure out our math homework*
   "I have to help my parents clean
   our apartment."

5. *repair my bedroom window*
   "My boss and her husband
   are coming for dinner."

6. *find one of my contact lenses*
   "I'm on my way to church."

7. *pick out new wallpaper*
   for my kitchen
   "I have to take care of my
   neighbor's daughter."

8. *fill out an application*
   for a bank loan
   "Both my children are
   home sick today."

9. *replace the cold water faucet*
   in my bathroom sink
   "I'm just about to take my wife
   to the hospital."

10.

DECISIONS

Read and practice.

Several years ago, my friends urged me not to quit my job at the post office. They told me that if I quit my job there, I would never find a better one.

I didn't follow their advice . . . and I'm glad that I didn't. I decided to quit my job at the post office, and found work as a chef in a restaurant downtown. I saved all my money for several years, and then opened a small restaurant of my own. Now my restaurant is famous, and people from all over town come to eat here.

I'm glad I didn't listen to my friends' advice. If I had listened to their advice, I probably never would have opened this restaurant and become such a success.

My brother thought I was crazy when I bought this car. He told me that if I bought this car, I'd probably have lots of problems with it.

I didn't follow his advice . . . and I'm really sorry I didn't. Since I bought this car two months ago, I've had to take it to the garage for repairs seven times.

I wish I had listened to my brother. If I had listened to him, I never would have bought such a "lemon"!

My ski instructor insisted that I was ready to try skiing down the mountain. I told him that I was really scared and that I thought I needed much more practice. He told me I was worrying too much, and that skiing down the mountain wasn't really very dangerous.

I decided to take his advice. I began to ski down the mountain, but after a few seconds, I lost my balance and crashed into a tree.

I wish I hadn't listened to my ski instructor. If I hadn't listened to him, I wouldn't be lying here in the hospital with my leg in a cast.

Do you remember a time when you had to make an important decision and people gave you lots of advice?

Talk with other students in your class about the advice people gave you and the decision you made:

What did people tell you?
Why did they tell you that?
Did you follow their advice?
What happened?
Do you think you made the right decision? Why or why not?

APPENDIX

Irregular Verbs

Irregular Verbs

be	was	been
become	became	become
begin	began	begun
bite	bit	bitten
blow	blew	blown
break	broke	broken
bring	brought	brought
build	built	built
buy	bought	bought
catch	caught	caught
choose	chose	chosen
come	came	come
cost	cost	cost
cut	cut	cut
do	did	done
draw	drew	drawn
drink	drank	drunk
drive	drove	driven
eat	ate	eaten
fall	fell	fallen
feed	fed	fed
feel	felt	felt
fight	fought	fought
find	found	found
fit	fit	fit
fly	flew	flown
forget	forgot	forgotten
forgive	forgave	forgiven
freeze	froze	frozen
get	got	gotten
give	gave	given
go	went	gone
grow	grew	grown
hang	hung	hung

have	had	had
hear	heard	heard
hide	hid	hidden
hit	hit	hit
hold	held	held
hurt	hurt	hurt
keep	kept	kept
know	knew	known
lead	led	led
leave	left	left
lend	lent	lent
let	let	let
light	lit	lit
lose	lost	lost
make	made	made
mean	meant	meant
meet	met	met
put	put	put
quit	quit	quit
read	read	read
ride	rode	ridden
ring	rang	rung
run	ran	run
say	said	said
see	saw	seen
sell	sold	sold
send	sent	sent
set	set	set
sew	sewed	sewed/sewn
shake	shook	shaken
shrink	shrank	shrunk
sing	sang	sung
sit	sat	sat
sleep	slept	slept

speak	spoke	spoken
spend	spent	spent
stand	stood	stood
steal	stole	stolen
sweep	swept	swept
swim	swam	swum
take	took	taken
teach	taught	taught
tell	told	told
think	thought	thought
throw	threw	thrown
understand	understood	understood
wake	woke	woken
wear	wore	worn
win	won	won
wind	wound	wound
write	wrote	written

Index

Word List

The number after each word indicates the page where the word first appears.

(n) = noun,   (v) = verb

This word list does not include words that first appeared in Books 1A, 1B, and 2A.

A

Abraham Lincoln   174
absent   154
accepted   179
accurately   110
acid   129
after school   125
agent   119
aggressive   138
airplane(s)   175
allergic   141
allowed   102
almost   118
all the time   156
all the way   119
ambulance   99
anniversary   178
annoyed   144
anthem   97
anyway   130
apology   130
application   193
argument   129
armchair   109
around the house   149
arrested   99
article   94
asleep   176
astronomy   141
attack   129
at that time   120
at the door   141
audience   153
auto mechanic   163

B

baby food   147
balance   188
bank loan   193
basketball coach   167
basketball player   167
bathtub   145
be allergic   141
be in a very good mood   125
bell(s)   96
bill(s)   105
birthmark(s)   120

bit   99
bite   99
bitten   98
blew   129
blown   129
blow up   129
box office   116
break into   142
break up   135
broke out   142
build   95
by   150
by ambulance   99
by then   100

C

cactus plant   155
came   153
capable   107
car accident   99
carve   97
cast   195
catch a bad cold   128
celebrate   149
championship   179
characteristic(s)   120
chased   127
check with   117
chemistry   129
chemistry set   159
Chicago   116
choking/choke   142
choose   99
chose   99
chosen   99
Christmas   97
church bell(s)   96
clearly   111
clip   101
clog(ging)   171
coach   167
come by   100
come to think of it   180
common cold   179
communicate/communicating   191
concentrate   149
concern   190

concerned   126
condition   139
confidently   124
congratulations   178
congressmen   139
considerate   109
contact lense(s)   193
contract   99
cookie jar   158
cotton   155
Could you please tell me   116
Could you possibly tell me   116
Could you tell me   116
couple   181
crash(ed)   195
crazy   95
cure   179
customer   155

D

Dad   115
daily   157
dance teacher   108
dangerous   176
daydream(ing)   189
deaf   119
deliver   169
depressed   157
design   95
detergent   105
dictionaries/dictionary   102
disappointed   137
discover(ed)   179
disease   155
dolphin(s)   177
don't worry about it   96
do the dishes   97
doubt   144
do you by any chance know   116
do you have any ideas   116
drank   127
dream   125
dress (v)   124
dressed up   141
driving test   124